LET'S FIND OUT! PRIMARY SOURCES

THE EMANCIPATION PROCLAMATION

MONIQUE VESCIA

Britannica®
Educational Publishing

IN ASSOCIATION WITH

ROSEN
EDUCATIONAL SERVICES

Published in 2017 by Britannica Educational Publishing (a trademark of Encyclopædia Britannica, Inc.) in association with The Rosen Publishing Group, Inc.
29 East 21st Street, New York, NY 10010

Distributed exclusively by Rosen Publishing.
To see additional Britannica Educational Publishing titles, go to rosenpublishing.com.

First Edition

Britannica Educational Publishing
J.E. Luebering: Executive Director, Core Editorial
Mary Rose McCudden: Editor, Britannica Student Encyclopedia

Rosen Publishing
Nicholas Croce and Amelie von Zumbusch: Editors
Nelson Sá: Art Director
Nicole Russo: Designer
Cindy Reiman: Photography Manager
Karen Huang: Photo Researcher

Library of Congress Cataloging-in-Publication Data

Names: Vescia, Monique, author.
Title: The Emancipation Proclamation / Monique Vescia.
Description: First edition. | New York : Britannica Educational Publishing in Association with
  Rosen Educational Services, 2017. | Series: Let's find out! Primary
  sources | Includes bibliographical references and index.
Identifiers: LCCN 2016021835| ISBN 9781508104056 (library bound)
  | ISBN 9781508104063 (pbk.) | ISBN 9781508103240 (6-pack)
Subjects: LCSH: United States. President (1861–1865 : Lincoln). Emancipation
  Proclamation—Juvenile literature. | Lincoln, Abraham, 1809–1865—Views on
  slavery—Juvenile literature. | United States—Politics and
  government—1861–1865—Juvenile literature. | Slaves—Emancipation—United
  States—Juvenile literature.
Classification: LCC E453 .V47 2016 | DDC 973.7/14—dc23
LC record available at https://lccn.loc.gov/2016021835

Manufactured in China

CONTENTS

WHAT IS A PRIMARY SOURCE?

How do people learn about the past? Students of history may examine both primary and secondary sources. A primary source is a record of a historical event made by someone who lived during that time. Official documents, recordings, memoirs, weather reports, and photographs all offer firsthand evidence of the past. A primary source may also be an artifact, such as a piece of clothing or pottery.

This photograph of the March on Washington, a 1963 protest for racial equality, is a primary source.

COMPARE AND CONTRAST

How is a primary source different from a secondary source? How are they similar?

A secondary source, such as a textbook, was created at a later time by someone who was not present at the time of the event. Secondary sources are often based on information gathered from primary sources.

One person's experience of an event may be very different from another's. Primary sources reflect these individual points of view and perspectives. Studying primary sources lets students and historians reach their own conclusions about the meaning of the past.

Studying a primary source can make history come alive.

SLAVERY

Primary sources are valuable for studying **slavery** in the United States. In the past, many societies had slavery. The trade of African slaves across the Atlantic Ocean began in the early 1500s. European ship captains bought people who had been forced into slavery from African traders. The ship captains

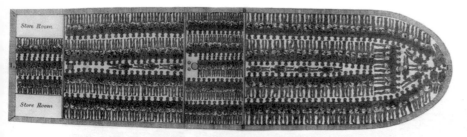

PLAN OF LOWER DECK WITH THE STOWAGE OF 292 SLAVES
130 OF THESE BEING STOWED UNDER THE SHELVES AS SHEWN IN FIGURE D & FIGURE 5.

Store Room

Store Room

PLAN SHEWING THE STOWAGE OF 130 ADDITIONAL SLAVES ROUND THE WINGS OR SIDES OF THE LOWER DECK BY MEANS OF PLATFORMS OR SHELVES
(IN THE MANNER OF GALLERIES IN A CHURCH) THE SLAVES STOWED ON THE SHELVES AND BELOW THEM HAVE ONLY A HEIGHT OF 2 FEET 7 INCHES
BETWEEN THE BEAMS: AND FAR LESS UNDER THE BEAMS. See Fig 1.

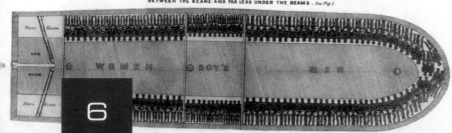

Humans were treated like cargo and packed tightly into slave ships. Many died at sea.

This color copy of the Emancipation Proclamation was printed in 1888.

then brought the slaves to the Americas, where Europeans had established colonies. Conditions on slave ships were terrible, and many people died. Those who survived were sold to people who forced them to work. The first enslaved Africans in what would become the United States arrived in the English colony of Virginia in 1619.

Accounts by people who were once slaves are a primary source for studying slavery. Ads looking for runaway slaves are, too. Another primary source is the Emancipation Proclamation. This document was issued during the American Civil War. It declared that the slaves in the Southern states were free.

Slave Labor in the South

At first, slavery was permitted in all the British colonies in North America. However, most slaves were on farms in the South. Southern plantation owners who grew tobacco and cotton purchased African slaves to work in their fields and harvest their crops. The Northern economy came to rely mostly on manufacturing. Paid workers kept mills and factories running.

In the 1700s some people in Britain came to believe that slavery was wrong. They started the abolitionist movement, an effort to end slavery.

Cotton was an important crop for the Southern states. The cotton was harvested by hand.

On plantations, slaves lived in simple wooden buildings, known as slave quarters.

THINK ABOUT IT

Compare the economies of the North and the South. Why do you think slavery lasted longer in the South?

By the time of the American Revolution, an abolitionist movement had started in the British colonies, too. Beginning with Vermont in 1777, slavery was banned in each of the northern states.

Large plantations in the Southern states still depended on slave labor. Even after the Atlantic slave trade was halted in 1808, children born to enslaved women became slaves themselves.

GROWING TENSIONS

Life for the slaves was very hard. They were forbidden to learn to read or write. Slaves could be bought and sold like animals, and families were split up. Slaves often suffered harsh punishments. Some escaped to the North, traveling in secret. They were helped by people who formed a system called the Underground Railroad.

In 1793 and 1850, the U.S. Congress passed laws called the Fugitive Slave Acts. These laws required that if escaped slaves were captured, they had to be returned to their owners in the South. The laws applied even

Harriet Tubman helped many slaves escape to the North.

Slave owners posted ads offering large rewards for the return of their "property."

$50 REWARD.

Ranaway from the subscriber on

TUESDAY MORNING, 26th ULTIMO,

My negro boy calling himself Severn Black. The said negro is about 5 feet six inches in height, chesnut color, has a scar on his upper lip, downcast countenance when spoken to, blink-eyed, showing a great deal of white, long bushy hair, is about twenty years old, had on when he left a blue fustian jacket, pantaloons of a greyish color, blue striped shirt, A BLACK SLOUCH HAT and shoes nearly worn out.

The above reward will be paid by me for the apprehension and delivery of the said negro in the County Jail at Princess Anne, Somerset county, Maryland. April 1, 1861. RICHARD E. SNELLING.

SOMERSET HERALD Print, Princess Anne, Md.

if a slave was captured in a free state, where slavery was outlawed. Free blacks could also be kidnapped and sold into slavery.

The Fugitive Slave Acts angered a lot of abolitionists in the North. Tensions between the northern and southern states would soon reach a boiling point.

THINK ABOUT IT

Slaves who attempted to escape were severely punished. If you were a slave, would you try to escape? Why or why not?

IN DEFENSE OF FREEDOM

Abolitionists fought against the Fugitive Slave Acts by helping slaves to escape. The abolitionists risked going to jail if they were caught breaking the law. They also spoke out against slavery in books, speeches, and more. Some clergymen criticized slavery in sermons.

In an 1838 speech, Southern-born abolitionist Angelina Grimké Weld talked about slavery. She said, "I know it has horrors that can never be

Angelina Grimké Weld fought for the rights of both slaves and women.

Frederick Douglass was both a brilliant speaker and a talented writer.

described.... I witnessed for many years its demoralizing influences, and its destructiveness to human happiness."

Former slave Frederick Douglass made powerful arguments against slavery in speeches and books. In *The Narrative of the Life of Frederick Douglass*, he described what he heard when slaves sang: "they breathed the prayer and complaint of souls boiling over with the bitterest **anguish**. Every tone was a testimony against slavery, and a prayer to God for deliverance from chains."

Slave States and Free States

As the United States gained more land to the west, Americans argued about whether to allow slavery in the new territories. Northerners wanted to stop the spread of slavery. The abolitionists formed a political group. They called themselves the Republican Party.

People in the South believed in "states' rights." They wanted each state to decide for itself whether or not to allow slavery. Most of the Southern economy depended on

As new territories were added to the United States, they had to decide whether or not to allow slavery.

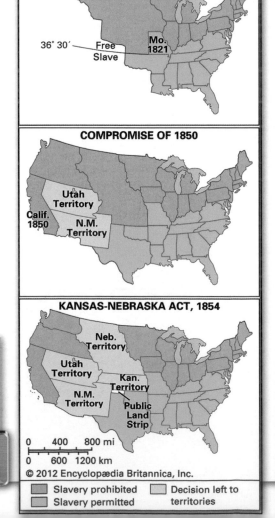

MISSOURI COMPROMISE, 1820

Me. 1820

36° 30′ — Free
Slave

Mo. 1821

COMPROMISE OF 1850

Utah Territory

Calif. 1850

N.M. Territory

KANSAS-NEBRASKA ACT, 1854

Neb. Territory

Utah Territory

Kan. Territory

N.M. Territory

Public Land Strip

| 0 | 400 | 800 mi |
| 0 | 600 | 1200 km |

© 2012 Encyclopædia Britannica, Inc.

Slavery prohibited · Decision left to territories
Slavery permitted

COMPARE AND CONTRAST

Why did the Southern states want to preserve slavery? Why did Northerners fight to end it?

cotton and tobacco, and those crops were picked by slaves.

One of the new U.S. territories was Kansas. There, proslavery and antislavery supporters fought and killed each other over the issue of slavery. This time of violence was called "Bleeding Kansas." Eventually, the abolitionists won. In 1861 Kansas joined the United States as a free state. But the violence pushed the United States ever closer to civil war.

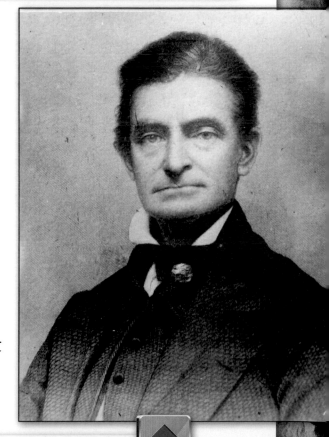

The abolitionist John Brown led a violent attack on a pro-slavery settlement in Kansas in 1856.

A Nation at War with Itself

Abraham Lincoln belonged to the Republican Party, which opposed slavery. When Lincoln was elected president in 1860, white Southerners were angry. Southern states decided to **secede** from the United States and form their own government. The Confederate States of America, or the Confederacy, elected Jefferson Davis as their president.

Abraham Lincoln was both loved and hated during his time in office.

Vocabulary

To **secede** means to formally withdraw from a group or organization.

Eventually, eleven states joined the Confederacy. The Northern states that remained loyal to the United States were called the Union. Some slave states on the border between the North and South did not secede. They remained a part of the Union. Many Americans still hoped to avoid going to war.

On April 12, 1861, Confederate troops attacked U.S. government forces at Fort Sumter in Charleston, South Carolina. The Confederates overpowered the fort and the U.S. forces surrendered. The attack on Fort Sumter sparked the beginning of the American Civil War. Fighting between Union and Confederate forces lasted from 1861 until 1865. The war claimed many hundreds of thousands of lives.

The Confederate capture of Fort Sumter started the Civil War.

DRAFTING THE EMANCIPATION PROCLAMATION

When the Civil War broke out, abolitionists wanted President Lincoln to emancipate, or free, all the slaves. Lincoln refused. He believed that his main purpose was to save the Union and to keep the states united. He worried that if he freed the slaves, border states such as Kentucky and Delaware might join the Confederacy.

Lincoln wrote a draft of the Emancipation Proclamation in July 1862. The war was less than

Most of the battles of the Civil War were fought in the Southern states.

This illustration from 1885 shows the Battle of Antietam.

a year old, and the Union armies had suffered serious defeats. Secretary of State William Seward worried that freeing the slaves might make people believe the Union couldn't win without the slaves' help. Seward convinced Lincoln to wait until a big Union victory.

After a string of losses, Union forces managed to hold back the Confederate army at the Battle of Antietam on September 17, 1862. This was Lincoln's chance. Five days later he released a **preliminary** version of the Emancipation Proclamation.

A Cause Worth Fighting For

The preliminary version of the Emancipation Proclamation declared that as of January 1, 1863, "all persons held as slaves within any state...in rebellion against the United States, shall be then...forever free." If the Confederate states did not stop their rebellion, then the proclamation would go into effect on January 1, 1863. On that

The original Emancipation Proclamation was written on a single piece of paper.

day, the slaves living in states at war with the Union would be free.

On January 1, 1863, President Lincoln issued the final version of the Emancipation Proclamation. The proclamation actually did not free any slaves. It did not apply to the border states, which were not in rebellion against the Union, and it was ignored by the Confederate states. However, the document changed the meaning of the war. The fight to save the Union became a fight for human freedom.

This painting honors Lincoln's role in the emancipation of the slaves.

THINK ABOUT IT

After they were freed, some slaves chose to remain on the plantations where they had worked. Why might they do that?

How the World Saw the War

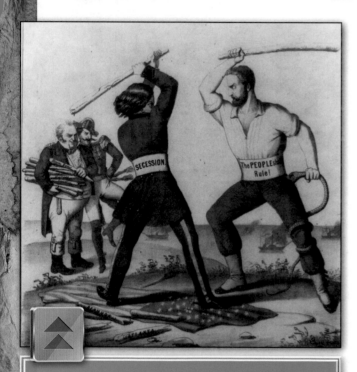

A cartoon shows the Union and the Confederacy fighting while England and France enjoy the show.

The Emancipation Proclamation made it clear that the Union was fighting to end slavery. And that would make all the difference. President Lincoln commanded the U.S. military to guard the freedom of the former slaves: "the executive government of the United States, including the [army and navy]...will recognize and maintain the freedom of [emancipated] persons."

The Confederacy, on the other hand, was fighting to preserve slavery, a practice that most civilized nations now considered **immoral**.

Near the beginning of the war, the South believed that European countries, such as Britain and France, would support them. The South thought that those countries needed the cotton from the Southern states. Some countries did consider supporting the Confederacy. However, after the Emancipation Proclamation was issued, most foreign support was with the North.

Union ships kept the Confederacy from exporting cotton to pay for the war.

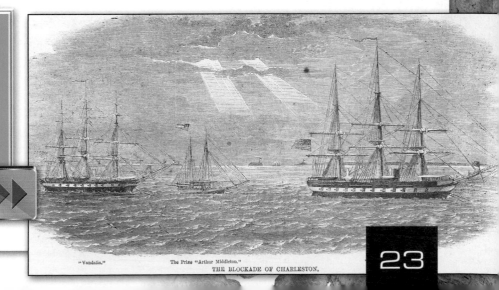

"Vandalia." The Prize "Arthur Middleton." THE BLOCKADE OF CHARLESTON,

JOINING THE RANKS

This drawing shows African American troops freeing slaves.

The Emancipation Proclamation declared the slaves in the Confederate states free. It also declared "that such persons of suitable condition will be received into the armed service of the United States." That meant that the emancipated slaves could serve in the Union army.

As soon as Union soldiers captured a region, the slaves were given their freedom. Almost 180,000 of the freed slaves joined the Union Army. Another 19,000 served in the navy.

THINK ABOUT IT

Both white and black Union soldiers were held prisoner during the Civil War. Which do you think the Confederates treated more harshly?

Members of the 4th U.S. Colored Infantry pose in Washington, D.C.

The Emancipation Proclamation said the Union would fight to end slavery. The emancipated slaves believed passionately in the cause they were fighting for. The new black recruits gave the North a real advantage in the war. They impressed their white commanders with their bravery in battle. However, throughout the war, black soldiers were not treated as equals to white soldiers.

A Long Road to Equality

On April 9, 1865, the Confederacy surrendered. Five days later, Abraham Lincoln was killed. Later that year, the 13th **Amendment** to the Constitution ended slavery throughout the United States. Additional amendments made African Americans U.S. citizens and gave black men the right to vote.

Before the war, the Southern economy and culture depended on

> **VOCABULARY**
>
> An **amendment** is a change or addition to a law.

> The 13th Amendment to the Constitution ended slavery throughout the United States.

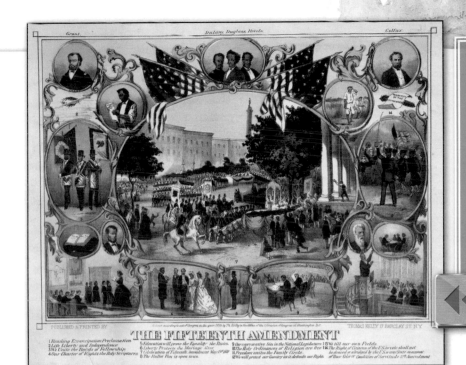

THE FIFTEENTH AMENDMENT

This illustration celebrates the 15th Amendment, which granted black men the right to vote.

slavery. Even after the slaves were freed, life was still difficult for most African Americans. Many whites did not see black people as their equals. They used violence to stop blacks in the South from voting and to keep them from making a new life for themselves.

The South was destroyed by the war and had to be rebuilt. During the Reconstruction period between 1865 and 1877, the North and South worked to put the United States back together. They often disagreed about exactly how to do that.

FOREVER FREE

An organization called the Freedmen's Bureau aided newly freed African Americans after the war. Millions of people needed food, access to medical care, and education. But Reconstruction failed to provide land for the freed slaves. Many became sharecroppers, part of a farming system that kept generations of African Americans in poverty. New laws called black codes restricted their activities and freedoms. The laws

Decades after the war, life had changed very little for many African Americans in the South.

Visitors view the original Emancipation Proclamation at the National Archives.

made sure that Southern whites stayed in control.

The Emancipation Proclamation is housed in the National Archives in Washington, D.C. It is one of the most important documents in the history of the United States. Yet more than 150 years after the proclamation was issued, the nation still struggles with the legacies of slavery. The Emancipation Proclamation was just the first step toward creating a fair society where all people share the same rights and privileges.

THINK ABOUT IT

Did the election of President Barack Obama, an African American, prove that the United States is a truly equal society? Why or why not?

Glossary

abolitionist Someone who is in favor of ending slavery.

artifact An object made by human beings.

ban To forbid, especially by law.

colony A distant territory belonging to or under the control of a country.

demoralize To weaken in spirit or discipline.

document A written or printed paper giving information about or proof of something.

draft A rough copy of a written document.

economy The way a country runs its industry, trade, and finance.

fugitive Someone who is running away, especially from the law.

legacy Something handed down from one person to another.

memoir A story of a personal experience.

plantation A large farm that is worked by laborers.

privilege A special right or advantage given to a person or a group.

rebel To be against or fight against authority.

recruit A newly enlisted member of the armed forces.

sharecroppers A farmer who works land for the owner in return for a share of the value of the crop.

testimony Firsthand evidence.

FOR MORE INFORMATION

Books

Blashfield, Jean F. *Slavery in America*. New York, NY: Children's Press, 2012.

Clark, Willow. *The True Story of the Emancipation Proclamation*. New York, NY: PowerKids Press, 2013.

Ford, Carin T. *The Underground Railroad and Slavery Through Primary Sources*. Berkeley Heights, NJ: Enslow, 2013.

Hall, Brianna. *Freedom from Slavery: Causes and Effects of the Emancipation Proclamation*. North Mankato, MN: Capstone Press, 2014.

Landau, Elaine. *Lincoln's Emancipation Proclamation: Would YOU Sign the Great Document?* Berkeley Heights, NJ: Enslow Elementary, 2015.

Websites

Because of the changing nature of internet links, Rosen Publishing has developed an online list of websites related to the subject of this book. This site is updated regularly. Please use this link to access the list:

http://www.rosenlinks.com/LFO/eman

INDEX